HEINEMANN
Profiles

Jesse Owens

An Unauthorized Biography

Philip Steele

Heinemann Library
Chicago, Illinois

Customer Service 888-454-2279

Visit our website at www.heinemannlibrary.com

Produced for Heinemann Library by Discovery Books
Edited by Patience Coster
Designed by Ian Winton
Originated by Dot Gradations
Printed and bound in Hong Kong/China

05 04 03 02 01
10 9 8 7 6 5 4 3 2 1

Library of Congress Cataloging-in-Publication Data
Steele, Philip, 1948-
    Jesse Owens / Philip Steele.
       p. cm. -- (Heinemann profiles)
    Includes bibliographical references (p.) and index.
    ISBN 1-58810-059-6 (library binding)
    1. Owens, Jesse, 1913---Juvenile literature. 2. Track and field athletes--United
States--Biography--Juvenile literature. [1. Owens, Jesse, 1913- 2. Track and field athletes.
3. Afro-Americans--Biography.] I. Title. II. Series.

GV697.O9 S84 2001
796.42'092--dc21
[B]
                                                              00-047261

Acknowledgments
The Publishers would like to thank the following for permission to reproduce photographs:
Hulton Getty, pp. 5, 9; Corbis, pp. 8, 45, 51; Bettman/Corbis, pp. 10, 15, 16, 17, 19, 21, 22, 27, 34, 35, 38, 39, 40, 42, 44; Cleveland Press Collection/Cleveland State University Library, pp. 12, 20; Hulton Deutsch Collection, p. 14; Peter Newark's Military Pictures, p. 24; Hulton Deutsch Collection/Corbis, pp. 25, 26; Hulton Getty/Allsport, p. 28; Popperfoto, pp. 29, 30, 31, 32, 33, 46, 48, 49; Keystone/Hulton Getty, p. 37.

Cover photograph reproduced with permission of Hulton Getty

Every effort has been made to contact copyright holders of any material reproduced in this book. Any omissions will be rectified in subsequent printings if notice is given to the Publisher.

Some words are shown in bold, **like this.** You can find out what they mean by looking in the glossary.

This is an unauthorized biography. The subject has not sponsored or endorsed this book.

CONTENTS

WHO WAS JESSE OWENS?

It was August, 1936. In the fashionable streets and cafés of Berlin, people spoke of just one subject—the **Olympic Games.** This ancient Greek festival of athletics, revived in 1896, is held every four years. It was about to be staged in Berlin, and it promised to be the biggest and most modern sporting event ever seen.

THE GAMES OF HATE?

At the time, Germany was ruled by the National Socialist German Workers' Party, known in short as the **Nazis.** Their **swastika** symbol appeared on red and white flags fluttering everywhere. The Nazi leader was Adolf Hitler (1889-1945), a ruthless and cunning politician. He had a burning hatred of people he thought were inferior to his German people—especially Jews, Slavs, Gypsies, and people of African descent.

As Hitler stepped out of his open-topped car to enter the Olympic stadium, a great roar went up. Thousands of voices shouted "Heil Hitler!" ("Hail Hitler!"), and a forest of arms shot into the air as the crowd made the Nazi salute.

To the athletes who had gathered there from all over the world to take part in the games, it was a chilling sound. Some of the athletes belonged to the same **ethnic groups** despised by the Nazis. Among them was a wiry and charming African-American track star named Jesse Owens.

RUNNING FOR FREEDOM

Jesse Owens displays perfect style at the Berlin Olympics.

Jesse Owens was one of the greatest athletes the world has ever seen. He was a natural athlete who ran and jumped with matchless speed and grace. Owens lived through a century of war and political violence. His life was greatly influenced by historical events beyond his control. He endured a poverty-stricken childhood and faced **racism** at home as well as abroad. Today, Owens is remembered with affection and admiration by people all over the world. At the Berlin Olympics that August in 1936, against great odds, Jesse Owens made history.

AN ALABAMA CHILDHOOD

Jesse was born far from Berlin, in Oakville, Alabama, on September 12, 1913. His parents, Henry and Emma, gave him the name James Cleveland Owens. However, most people called him simply "J.C."

BLACK AND WHITE

At that time, Alabama had a population of more than two million people. About forty-three percent of the people were of African-American descent, and most of the rest were of European descent. Jesse's grandparents had been born as **slaves.** Slavery was abolished in the United States in 1865.

What is racism?

Many people used to believe that human beings could be divided into groups called "races" according to their physical appearances. They placed great emphasis on small physical differences between **ethnic groups.**

Racists believe that such racial divisions are important. Even worse, they believe that some races are superior to others. During the 1920s and 1930s, racist ideas were common among white people all over the world.

However, advances in the study of **genetics** proved that such divisions are not meaningful. The genetic differences between the ethnic groups are very small. It makes much more sense to say that there is only one "race" in the world—the human race.

By the time Jesse was born, African Americans were legally free. However, in many parts of the United States, especially in the south, society remained **segregated** or divided. This meant that African Americans were not treated the same as their white neighbors. Schools were also segregated, and black children like Jesse were given few chances in life.

LIVING OFF THE LAND

During the 1900s, 83 percent of the people in Alabama lived in the country. The chief crop in the region was cotton, which grows well in the hot summer sunshine of the south. However, since 1909, many Alabama farmers had become fearful for their livelihood because a destructive pest called the boll weevil threatened the cotton crop. Like most of his neighbors, Henry Owens was a **sharecropper,** a kind of tenant farmer. His small timber house was owned by the landlord, and the family's rent was paid in the form of a large share of the crop. The family had to survive on the money brought in by the remainder of the share. It was a hard life for Jesse, who was the youngest of ten children. He was a rather sickly boy who suffered several times from **pneumonia** and **bronchitis.** There was no money to buy medicine, and his parents had to nurse him through several serious illnesses.

OFF TO SCHOOL

Jesse's mother, Emma, was determined that her children would make successes of their lives. At the age of six, Jesse went to school. In those days there were no school buses, so Jesse faced a very long walk to the little school. It was a simple hut used as a Baptist chapel on Sundays. There he soon learned to read and write.

In the spring and fall there was so much work to do on the farm that the children of the **sharecroppers** had to stay home from school to help out in the fields. It was tough, back-breaking work under a blazing hot sun. There was little machinery on farms at that time, just muscle power. In the southern states, mules were still widely used to plow the land.

Many African Americans in the South faced poverty and racism. However, shared problems often led to strong community values and family ties.

Sharecroppers worked hard but received a tiny share of the profits.

GAMES AND RUNNING

However, it was not all hard work, and Jesse would later remember his early childhood as a happy one. Jesse loved to swim and play outside with his friends. Even then, it was clear that he was a fast runner—just as his father had been in his day. Jesse loved running because of the sense of freedom it gave him as he ran around, exploring the Alabama countryside. However, his days as a country boy would soon come to an end.

"I always loved running. . . . You could go in any direction, fast or slow as you wanted, fighting the wind if you felt like it…"

Jesse Owens, on his childhood

A MOVE TO THE CITY

When Jesse was nine, the Owens family made a big decision. The idea first came from Jesse's sister Lillie, who had moved to Cleveland, Ohio. She wrote to tell them that this northern city was the place to get ahead in life, a place to leave the poverty of the **sharecropping** life far behind.

Henry Owens was all too aware that his skills as a farmer would be of little use in the big city, but Emma persuaded him that it was time for a change. They had nothing to lose. With mixed feelings, the Owens family headed north by train, bound for Cleveland's East Side.

CITY OF STEEL

Cleveland was a sprawling industrial city, built where the Cuyahoga River flows into Lake Erie. One reason for the city's success was that it provided

Jesse Owens was part of a large family. This photograph was taken in 1936. Jesse is in the back row, on the left.

a link between the iron ore-producing regions around Lake Superior and the coal mines of Ohio, Pennsylvania, and West Virginia.

Industry in Cleveland centered around steel manufacturing. Henry and Jesse's older brothers found work in the steel mills. Emma worked hard cleaning houses and doing other people's laundry.

Cleveland was a rapidly growing city that had attracted many **immigrants** from other parts of the world. Its population included Irish, Germans, Italians, Jews, Central Europeans, and many African Americans escaping the southern countryside, just like the Owens family.

Jesse soon learned one difference between Ohio and Alabama. His new elementary school was **integrated.** For the first time, he would be going to school with both black and white students.

"J.C." BECOMES JESSE

It was at elementary school that Jesse was first called "Jesse." When he hesitantly told his new teacher that he was called "J.C." she misunderstood and registered him as "Jesse" Owens. The name would stick for the rest of his life.

Part-time jobs

Jesse soon settled down in his new home, although he still suffered from bouts of illness. He helped the family bring in some money by doing all kinds of part-time jobs. He delivered groceries and helped out at a shoe-repair shop.

Riley to the rescue

It was when Jesse moved up to Fairmount Junior High School that he began to make his mark as an athlete. The man who first spotted his talent was a square-jawed Irish-American named Charles Riley, the track coach at Fairmount. The two got along very well, and Jesse called him "Pop."

Jesse Owens and coach Charles Riley soon developed a strong respect for each other.

Riley, who often wore short-sleeved shirts with a bow tie, was always out on the track with the teenager. Riley made Jesse run, run, and run some more. He made Jesse try out the 440-yard (402-meter) and the 100-yard (91-meter) sprints. He introduced him to hurdles, the long jump, and the high jump. Jesse became stronger and fitter. Riley encouraged the relaxed, natural style of running that would become Jesse's trademark.

> "I got up with the sun, ate my breakfast even before my mother and sister and brothers, and went to school, winter, spring, and fall alike, to run and jump and bend my body this way and that. . . ."
>
> Jesse Owens, on training

In 1928, Riley introduced Jesse to an athlete named Charlie Paddock, who had been a gold medalist at the 1920 **Olympic Games.** Jesse was inspired. He could already run 100 yards (91 meters) in 11 seconds and was selected for the Fairmount track team. He became determined to be a great athlete one day, too.

In 1929, a car hit Jesse's father, breaking his leg. He couldn't work and soon lost his job at the steel mill. Henry Owens' chance of finding new work was slim. His eyesight was failing. Worse, the **economy** crashed that same year. During the years that followed, which came to be known as the Great Depression, many people in the United States and around the world became unemployed and suffered great hardship.

Jesse's family made a difficult but wise choice. Jesse should not quit his schooling now in order to help support the family. In the long term, they decided, it would be better for him to finish his education.

RISING STAR

Jesse Owens was growing up. He was popular, amusing, well-dressed, and hard-working, too. One of his best friends at Fairmount Junior High School was an attractive, lively girl named Minnie Ruth Solomon. She, too, was African American and from a very similar background to Jesse. The two young people were immediately attracted to each other.

Their friendship continued after Jesse went to high school. In 1930, when he was seventeen, Jesse enrolled at Cleveland's East Technical High School. He had never been interested in book work, and the Technical School was a place to learn job skills rather than academics. It was a good place for Jesse to continue his passion for track.

Jesse Owens, age 19, represents Cleveland's East Technical High School in 1932.

In 1932, sixteen-year-old Minnie Ruth became pregnant. At first, the Owens and Solomon families were furious with nineteen-year-old Jesse. After all, these young people still had their own lives to sort out. How could they be ready for family responsibilities? Minnie Ruth left school and worked as a beautician in a shop. She stayed at her parents' house, where Jesse was no longer welcome. That summer, she had a baby daughter and named her Gloria.

THE TECHNICAL STUDENT

At the Technical School, coach Edgar Weil soon realized he had a very talented student in his care. Jesse decided to concentrate on track rather than on basketball or football. He was pleased when the school allowed Charles Riley to continue coaching him. Jesse became the star of the school track team and was very popular with the other students.

Jesse proudly shows his medals to his mother in 1933.

Top competition

Jesse was now seen as a rising star in the world of American track and field. He was also a contender for serious international competition. During the summer of 1932, Jesse took part in the U.S. **Olympic** trials, which were held at Northwestern University in Evanston, Illinois. He lost the 220-yard (201-meter) and 100-yard (91-meter) sprints to Ralph Metcalfe, another great sprinter who eventually became his close friend.

Jesse Owens was not chosen for the U.S. Olympic team that competed at the Los Angeles games that year. But still, he was now competing at the highest level and was learning all the time.

By 1933, Jesse was increasingly dazzling the experts. In May of that year, he leapt an amazing 24 ft., $3^1/2$ in. (7.4 meters) in the long jump at the Ohio State Interscholastic event.

FAME IN CHICAGO

The following month, Jesse competed at the National Interscholastic Championships in Chicago. Jesse's performances electrified the radio announcers. He jumped 24 ft., 9⅝ in. (7.5 meters) in the long jump, then tied the world 100-yard (91-meter) record with a time of 9.4 seconds. He also set a new world record of 20.7 seconds in the 220-yard (201-meter) race.

Jesse had achieved fame before his twentieth birthday. Back in Cleveland, he was given a hero's welcome. He rode through the streets in a parade with his proud parents and coach Charles Riley. Ray Miller, the mayor, congratulated him on his impressive achievements.

Cleveland mayor Ray Miller congratulates Jesse Owens on his amazing performance in Chicago.

Minnie Ruth was proud of Jesse, too. Her parents finally agreed to allow him to visit her and the baby. Jesse took a job at a gas station to bring in some extra money. The future was looking bright for Jesse.

THE RECORD BREAKER

The next step for Jesse Owens was to join a university team. During the 1930s, the only way an athlete could get to the **Olympics** was through the university circuit as an **amateur.** Many colleges and universities would postpone academic qualifications if the athletes could pass a basic entry test. Twenty-eight colleges offered Jesse a place as a student, even though his high school grades had not been very good. However, Jesse was tested and accepted at his first-choice school, Ohio State, in Columbus.

THE FRESHMAN

It was understood that Jesse would concentrate on track and field, but he did have to do academic work, too. Jesse always found that hard since he had never been given the educational background he needed. Because he was the son of a poor African-American **sharecropper,** most of his teachers had never expected him to go to college.

Jesse's friends warned him to expect **racism** at college, and he found it. Because he was black, he was not allowed to live on **campus.** He could not share a ride to a track meet with his white teammates or even use the same shower afterward.

This was no surprise to Jesse. But even though he had experienced attitudes like these all his life, it

Segregation was widespread in the United States during the 1930s. This photo shows a segregated drinking fountain.

must have been hard for the twenty-year-old freshman to be treated as inferior one minute and as a great athlete the next. However, Jesse did meet many kind people at college and was always good at making friends.

Jesse got a part-time job at Ohio's State House in Columbus. He worked as an elevator operator and later as a messenger. He earned $3 a day and was known and liked by everybody.

Training for success

The university track coach was Larry Snyder, who took over where Charles Riley had left off. The training program was tough and well-planned. At the 1934 Amateur Athletic Union (AAU) meet in New York, Jesse completed a long jump of 25 ft., 3¹/₄ in. (7.7 meters). He was now ready to compete with his greatest rivals, Ralph Metcalfe and Eulace Peacock.

Pure magic

On May 25, 1935, Jesse Owens took to the track in Ann Arbor, Michigan, for the Big Ten Championship meet. A crowd of some 12,000 spectators packed the stands. Both Jesse and Larry Snyder must have been anxious, because Jesse had hurt himself falling down the stairs just a week before.

Jesse's remarkable feats at Ann Arbor were followed by more athletic achievements.

At 3:15 P.M., Jesse again tied the world record for 100 yards (91 meters), with a time of 9.4 seconds. At 3:25 P.M., he jumped 26 ft., 8¹/₄ in. (8.1 meters) in the long jump, setting a world record that no one would break for another 25 years. At 3:45 P.M., he ran 220 yards (201 meters) in 20.3 seconds. This, too, was a world record and included the fastest ever 200-meter (218-yard) race. At 4:00 P.M., Jesse shattered another record, the 220-yard (201-meter) low hurdles, with a time of 22.6 seconds. The events of that day, which took place in the span of less than an hour, remain some of the most extraordinary athletic achievements ever.

> "I could hardly go to my mark at the start. . . but when the starter said 'Get Set' my pain left."
>
> Jesse Owens, recalling his Ann Arbor success

COMING DOWN TO EARTH

Fame did not bring Jesse instant fortune, nor did it solve all his problems. The AAU was questioning his **amateur** status because of his paid job with the Ohio State House. The university complained that his academic work was not good enough. The strain was beginning to affect his running. At home, Minnie Ruth was worried that celebrity was taking Jesse away from her and Gloria. Minnie Ruth and Jesse decided to get married.

Jesse Owens and Minnie Ruth Solomon were married on July 5, 1935.

Inspiration in sports

Racism in sports was common. These Chicago Giants team members played in an all African-American league. Baseball was not **integrated** until 1947.

Many young people, especially those raised in poverty, dream of becoming professional athletes. But the dream often has more meaning for African Americans. Faced with the indignities of **racism** and **segregation,** African Americans came to see sports as a source of inspiration. During the early part of the century, for instance, the victories of boxers Jack Johnson and Joe Louis—as well as the astounding performance in Berlin by Jesse Owens— proved to them that black men could compete against whites—and win. The boxing ring and

running track became stand-ins for other places in society that excluded African Americans. The same was true when Jackie Robinson became the first African American to play for a major league baseball team in 1947. Before then, there were separate leagues for African-American players. When Robinson "broke the color barrier" by joining the all-white Brooklyn Dodgers, African Americans from all across the country became instant Dodgers fans to show their support.

Sports and race

W. Montague Cobb, an African-American professor of **anatomy** at Howard University in Washington, D.C., was fascinated by claims by racist coaches that African Americans were superior on the track because of physical differences or because of other, social, causes. In 1936, after carrying out a detailed physical examination of Jesse Owens, he published an article in the *Journal of Health and Physical Education.* Cobb wrote that there was no significant difference in performance between blacks and whites and that there were no relevant physical differences. All that counted, he decided, was motivation and the influences with which the athlete had grown up.

The nazis in germany

During the 1930s in Germany, **racism** was the official policy of the ruling **Nazi** Party. The country had been defeated by the United States and its allies in World War I, and many Germans still felt bitter and humiliated. They were suffering from **economic** hardship as well.

Germany's leader, Adolf Hitler, thought he would gain supporters by blaming the country's troubles on the **ethnic groups** he hated. He claimed that the northern Europeans belonged to a superior race that he called "Aryan" and that people of other races were sub-human.

Adolf Hitler preached his bizarre theories of "racial purity" at huge rallies across Germany.

To boycott the games?

When it was announced that the 1936 **Olympic Games** would be held in Nazi Germany, many Americans did not want to send a team to compete. By then, the world knew about Nazi **persecution** of the Jews. In 1933, the AAU had already voted to **boycott** the games.

A banner on Nazi headquarters in 1935 reads: "In defending myself against the Jew I strive in the work of the Lord."

Some African Americans believed that a boycott of the Olympics would be pure **hypocrisy.** After all, they said, the white sports **establishment** in the United States was racist itself because of the way it treated its own African-American athletes.

In the end, the U.S. Olympic Committee decided to send a team. Sports, they argued, had nothing to do with politics. This was an opinion that Jesse Owens always supported. The Olympic trials were held in July 1936 in New York City. Jesse won the 100-meter (109-yard) and 200-meter (218-yard) races as well as the long jump. This time, Jesse was certain of his place on the U.S. Olympic team.

Beating Hitler

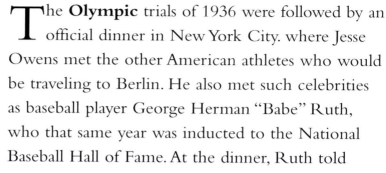

The **Olympic** trials of 1936 were followed by an official dinner in New York City. where Jesse Owens met the other American athletes who would be traveling to Berlin. He also met such celebrities as baseball player George Herman "Babe" Ruth, who that same year was inducted to the National Baseball Hall of Fame. At the dinner, Ruth told Owens that the secret of success in any sport was to *know* that you were going to win—it was all down to self-confidence. Jesse paid close attention.

On the ocean voyage to Germany, Jesse Owens continued training.

The mid-1930s was the great age of ocean liners, and the U.S. Olympic team traveled to Europe across the Atlantic on a luxurious ship called the *Manhattan*. The sea voyage lasted a week, and Owens watched his diet and made sure he kept training.

To Berlin

The *Manhattan* docked at Bremerhaven in northern Germany on June 24, 1936, and the U.S. team continued on to the capital by train. They, along with athletes from fifty-one other nations, checked in at Berlin's **Olympic village.** Training now began in earnest. Owens's university coach, Larry Snyder, showed up to keep an eye on him and offer advice to the U.S. Olympic coaches.

IN THE PUBLIC EYE

An impressive new stadium, the *Olympia-Stadion*, had been built in Berlin's western suburbs for the occasion. It was designed to accommodate the expected daily crowds of about 70,000 to 110,000 people. The Berlin Olympics were the first to be televised. Hitler hired German filmmaker Leni Riefenstahl to make the powerful official film of the games, *Olympische Spiele 1936*. The film was also shown under the title *Olympiad*.

German filmmaker Leni Riefenstahl (center) made a powerful record of the 1936 Olympics.

Propaganda

Adolf Hitler had intended the **Olympic Games** to be a showcase of **Nazi** Germany, a brilliant example of **propaganda** designed to demonstrate to the world the "superiority" of the Aryan race. Loyal Nazis with adoring faces lined the streets to watch Hitler drive by.

The American Olympic team takes a stroll through Berlin. Owens is third from the right.

Hitler decided to show a phony, less threatening face to the world for the Olympics. Anti-Jewish posters were taken down, and some part-Jewish athletes were even allowed to represent Germany. Many visitors were fooled.

The flame is lit

The Games began on August 1, 1936, with the lighting of the **Olympic flame** by a torch brought all the way from Greece, the ancient home of the Olympic Games. Hitler stood in the official box with other leading Nazis. They included Hermann Goering, head of the German air force; and Joseph Goebbels, who was Hitler's chief of propaganda.

The Olympic flame arrives at the packed Berlin stadium, beneath the swastika banners of Nazi Germany.

Hitler said that the Americans should be ashamed of themselves for allowing African Americans to win their medals for them. He also said that he would never shake hands with African-American athletes. It had been the practice for the leader of the hosting country to shake hands with medal winners. But the International Olympic Committee (IOC) stopped this practice for the 1936 Games so the awkward situation never came up.

Powerful as Hitler was, he couldn't stop the German people from liking Jesse Owens. Many people admired his charm, patience, and easy manner.

It cannot have been an easy time for any of the athletes, let alone Owens and the other African Americans representing the United States. Owens did not dwell too much on the politics of it all. He had come to compete, and that had to be his only concern if he was to succeed.

TAKE YOUR MARKS!

The long-awaited Games had begun. First came the **heats,** which determined who would compete in the finals. Owens got off to a flying start with a 100-meter (109-yard) sprint in 10.3 seconds, tying his own record. In the next heat, he shortened it to 10.2 seconds, but the time was disqualified because the wind had been in his favor. On the next day, he ran the 100-meter (109-yard) semifinals in a respectable 10.4 seconds. In the final, Owens stormed home with another 10.3. He was running his best, and the crowd roared its appreciation.

> "I was going to fly. I was going to stay up in the air forever."
> Jesse Owens, on his record-breaking long jump

The following day were the 200-meter (218-yard) heats, followed by the long jump. Owens got through the sprint in record-breaking time, but he ran into trouble with the long jump. German athlete Lutz Long gave him helpful advice, and they became friends. The two men ended up competing for the gold medal in

Jesse Owens streaks to victory in the 200-meter race.

the long jump. The winner? Jesse Owens, with a record-breaking 26 ft., 8¼ in. (8.1 meters). Hitler must have been growing more and more frustrated. Not only had his German hero lost, but he had publicly shown the world his affection and admiration for an African American.

Owens is congratulated by Swedish athlete Lennart Strandberg after winning the 100- meter sprint.

The 200-meter (218-yard) final brought further humiliation for Hitler and the **Nazis.** At the end of it, Owens was again number one after winning the gold medal with an **Olympic** record of 20.7 seconds.

Owens had finished his scheduled events, but the U.S. Olympic officials wanted him and Ralph Metcalfe to run in the 4x100-meter (109-yard) relay in place of the selected runners. Owens wanted them to run, but he was overruled.

"It seems to take an eternity, yet it is all over before you can think of what's happening."

Jesse Owens, on the 100-meter sprint

Jesse Owens wears his gold medal in the ceremony for the long jump at Berlin.

Owens and the other three team members won a gold medal for the United States with an outstanding time of 39.8 seconds.

END OF THE RACES

Finally, the Games were over, and the crowds of international visitors and journalists left the leafy avenues of Berlin. The teams left, too. The stadium lay empty. There would be no more **Olympic Games** until 1948, because not long after the 1936 Games, Adolf Hitler's policies led to world war in Europe.

Meanwhile, the AAU had arranged further meets across northern Europe for the U.S. track team. They competed in Dresden, Cologne, Prague, Bochum, and London. Stockholm was next on the schedule, but Owens, exhausted, said it was time to go home. Larry Snyder agreed, but the AAU was furious because Owens was its star attraction. In spite of their protests, Owens sailed for the United States aboard the *Queen Mary*.

"As a **Negro**, I am proud of those black athletes who comported themselves so honorably in sportsmanship at Berlin."
A letter from F. V. Harris to London's *Daily Telegraph*, 1936

The Berlin legacy

Jesse Owens achieved amazing feats in Berlin, giving one of the most remarkable Olympic performances of all time. More importantly, in spite of **Nazi** claims to Aryan superiority, he left the world with a series of unforgettable images of African-American excellence and beauty.

For many people, the photos of Jesse Owens embracing Lutz Long seemed to symbolize the true Olympic spirit. These images remained in the public memory long after Long was killed in World War II a few years later. They even survived the city in which the games were held. The Berlin that Owens visited in the summer of 1936 was destroyed by bombing by the time the war ended in 1945.

German long jumper Lutz Long had not been afraid to show his friendship for Jesse Owens in front of the Nazi crowds.

THE HOMECOMING

When the *Queen Mary* sailed into harbor, Jesse Owens found that he was one of the most famous men in the United States. He was welcomed back by his proud mother, Emma, and his jubilant wife, Minnie Ruth. There were exciting victory parades and public honors in Cleveland and Columbus, Ohio.

Emma and Minnie Ruth welcome home the conquering hero.

Back in New York, Owens met up with his teammates from Berlin for the city's traditional **tickertape** parade. As it did after every **Olympic Games,** paper and confetti showered down from Manhattan's skyscrapers like a blizzard of snow.

SOUR NOTES

Already, however, some parts of the victory were beginning to seem a little hollow. There was no official message of congratulations from the office of President Roosevelt, nor was there an invitation to meet with him at the White House. These were other traditions that usually took place after the Olympics.

The AAU, holding a grudge, suspended Owens from membership for refusing to go to the Stockholm meet. In those days, **amateur** status was important to athletes, but it meant they couldn't hold paying jobs. This was fine for athletes who were wealthy to start with. But for people from a poor background, like Owens, making a living was important.

A CHANGE OF DIRECTION

Owens was offered advice by many people, including his coach, Larry Snyder. Owens had found a new friend, too, in African-American dancer and entertainer Bill "Bojangles" Robinson, who met him on his return. Robinson introduced Owens to **agent** Marty Forkins. There was talk of large amounts of money and of film offers in Hollywood.

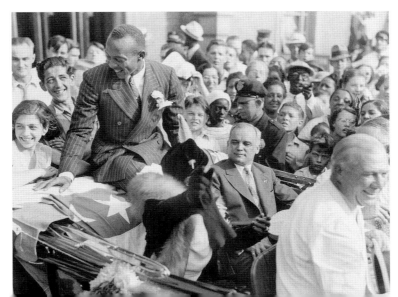

Crowds jostle to get a glimpse of America's most famous athlete during his victory parade.

> "I've lost six pounds (2.7 kilograms) being circused and pushed all over Europe. I'm burned out and tired of being treated like a head of cattle."
> Jesse Owens, on why he became a professional athlete

Such deals were not as **lucrative** as those signed by successful athletes today, but they were huge by 1930s standards. Owens could hardly believe the possibilities.

Owens decided to sign a contract with **agent** Marty Forkins. By doing so he was finally breaking his ties with the AAU. Owens did indeed have to quit the amateur athletics circuit, and, tragically, this proved to be the end of his career as a serious athlete.

In truth, Owens was burned out. He was exhausted by the tension of the Berlin **Olympics,** by the way in which African–American athletes were treated in the United States, and by his new–found celebrity.

An inspiration

However, the story of Jesse Owens the athlete was far from over. During the 1930s and 1940s, countless young athletes were inspired by his example. One such youth was Harrison Dillard, who watched Owens's 1936 victory parade in Cleveland, wide-eyed in wonder. Dillard grew up to become a world–class athlete, winning many races between the years 1947 and 1952.

JESSE TAKES TO POLITICS

Jesse Owens was no politician, but he did want to make things better for people. He became a paid campaign speaker for Alf Landon, the Republican governor of Kansas. In 1936, Landon was challenging Franklin D. Roosevelt for the presidency. Owens turned out to be a fluent and accomplished speaker in public, and his speeches were received well. However, Landon still lost the election.

Harrison Dillard runs the hurdles in 1948. He was one of many rising stars who followed the example of Jesse Owens.

THE SHOWMAN

Jesse Owens tried to organize a two-man race in Cuba on December 26, 1936. His opponent was to be ace sprinter Conrado Rodrigues. When the event was canceled, Owens agreed to run against a racehorse instead. He won and took the money. Owens went on to do more exhibitions like this and came to be billed, like some circus act, as "the Ebony Antelope." To some people, it seemed these races were unworthy of a great **Olympic** athlete.

Jesse Owens runs against a horse in 1948 and wins.

BANDS, BASKETBALL, AND BOXERS

Jesse Owens was always a showman. In 1937 he got a contract as a bandleader from Bill "Bojangles" Robinson and went on tour. Owens looked great, but he wasn't really musical. He made good money for a few months. Then he set up touring basketball

Jesse Owens met with boxer Joe Louis in 1935.

teams that performed exhibition matches across the United States. He ran, too, against leading baseball stars and even against champion boxer Joe Louis.

TIME TO RETHINK

Owens was soon in serious financial trouble. The big money that had been promised in 1936 never really materialized. He took a job as a playground director in Cleveland. Then, in 1938, he became manager of a dry-cleaning business, but it collapsed and left him $114,000 in debt.

Back in Europe, war had broken out against **Nazi** Germany in 1939. However, it was 1941 before the United States was drawn into the conflict.

These were troubled times for the Owens family, too. Owens's mother died in March 1940, and his father died just six months later. Jesse and Minnie Ruth felt the loss deeply, but they were now parents to two more daughters of their own. Marlene was born in 1937 and Beverly in 1940. The couple found consolation in family life.

Jesse Owens decided that it was time to try again to finish the university degree he had abandoned before Berlin. He did some track coaching when he was back there, too. However, by 1941, Jesse decided that he was never going to complete his degree and he left the university.

WAR WORK

In late 1941, the United States entered World War II against Germany and Japan. Owens now took on important war work with the Civilian Defense Office, organizing a national physical fitness program. Later, the government offered him a job with the Ford Motor Company, which was at the time making cars for the war effort. Owens became a **personnel officer,** and his duties included dealing with African-American car workers in Detroit. He negotiated with **trade unions** and sorted out any problems faced by the workers.

Jesse Owens continued to start up new businesses. He tried again with dry cleaning in 1954.

1945

In 1945, World War II ended. American, British, French, and Russian troops occupied Germany. The long years of war had put an end to international athletics, including the **Olympic Games.** Now that the war was over, it was time to plan for new Games. Owens was still in good shape, but by now he was too old to compete in the Olympics.

As the war ended, so did Owens's contract with Ford. Ever the showman, he worked for a time as a disc jockey, with his own radio jazz show. At the same time, he was working on other projects.

Sports and politics

Although we may think that political quarrels and accusations of cheating are new in sports, they were common even in ancient Greece. The Berlin Olympics were not the only contest to be overshadowed by a political cloud. During the Munich Olympics of 1972, members of the Israeli team were taken hostage by Palestinian terrorists. Nine hostages, four terrorists, and a policeman were killed in the shoot-out that followed. Many black athletes **boycotted** the 1976 Montreal Olympics because of the IOC's tolerance of **racist** South Africa. The United States and West Germany boycotted the 1980 Moscow Olympics because of their governments' outrage at the invasion and occupation of Afghanistan by the Soviet Union in 1979. At the Sydney Olympics in 2000, Australian Aborigines protested about racist laws in Australia.

MAN OF BUSINESS

Jesse Owens decided to start a **public relations** company after the war, and in 1946 he became head of sales for the Leo Rose Sporting Goods Company. Owens and his family moved to Chicago in 1949.

THE TELEVISION AGE

During the 1950s, the new medium of television overshadowed radio. With the birth of television came the rapid growth of the advertising industry. Owens took to it naturally and was soon promoting products on TV. His name and achievements were well remembered by the public. Owens took part in speaking engagements for his **sponsors,** in which he talked to groups of business people, religious organizations, sporting associations, and other groups. He was an outstanding success.

AN AMBASSADOR

Owens always liked to emphasize that anyone could make it in the United States, just as he had. His message was popular with his conservative audiences. It was were also popular with Republican politicians such as

Dwight D. Eisenhower, the wartime general who had led the Allied attack on Hitler between 1943 and 1945.

Eisenhower was U.S. president between 1953 and 1961, a period of growing tension between the United States and the Soviet Union known as the Cold War. Eisenhower sent Owens as a "goodwill ambassador" around the world. He traveled to India, Malaysia, and the Philippines. Wherever he went, Owens charmed and inspired many young people with his descriptions of sports and the American way of life. He was described as a "professional good example."

AWARDS AND ACTIVISM

Owens's athletic achievements were not forgotten at home. In 1949, *Ebony* magazine voted him the greatest African-American athlete of all time. The next year, the Associated Press voted him the greatest track and field athlete of the first half of the twentieth century.

Owens devoted a lot of his time to the support of track and field in Chicago. He served as Secretary of the Illinois State Athletic Commission from 1952–55. He also helped African-American youngsters at the Southside Boys' Club. In 1956, Owens organized a Junior Sports Jamboree for the Youth Commission in Illinois.

WHERE DO YOU STAND, BROTHER?

During the 1950s and 1960s, historical events again affected the life of Jesse Owens. Once again, the issue was race. African-Americans were pushing against the old injustices of racial **discrimination** and **segregation,** which still persisted in the south and in parts of the northern United States.

CIVIL RIGHTS?

A civil rights movement grew up under the inspired leadership of Dr. Martin Luther King Jr. His powerful message of non-violence won over many white people to his cause. In 1963, King organized a great march in Washington D.C. It had a massive impact in the United States and around the world.

Civil rights marchers take to the streets of New York City. Jesse Owens had little sympathy with protest movements.

Jesse Owens, who had never had much interest in political protest, offered no active support for the civil rights movement. He believed that African Americans should improve their own lives through enterprise and hard work. Money brought power, he reasoned. It was a simplistic view that did not reflect the reality of life for most African Americans living in the United States.

Owens's message was conservative, too, and these were not conservative times. Around the world, people of all races were trying to create a better world through new social attitudes, new music,

Martin Luther King Jr. speaks of an end to racism in June of 1966.

new fashion, and a new sense of justice.

In 1968, Jesse Owens finally realized that he had lost touch with his African-American roots. That year, Martin Luther King Jr. was killed. Black America rose in protest, rioting and burning cities from Los Angeles to Washington D.C. The Mexico City **Olympic Games** took place against this backdrop.

To mexico city

Owens, a fund-raiser for the U.S. Olympic Committee, went to Mexico City unaware of the storm that was brewing back home and among the Olympic athletes. Most of the African-American athletes wanted to make some form of public protest. They wanted to communicate their bitterness about the way African-American athletes were still treated in the United States.

OLYMPIC PROTEST

They also wanted to join other African-American competitors in expressing their outrage that the IOC supported the campaign to allow South Africa to compete at the games. At that time, South Africa was ruled by a **racist** white government that refused to grant some basic freedoms, like the vote, to citizens of African or Asian descent.

Tommie Smith and John Carlos raise their fists and bow their heads at the 1968 Mexico City Olympics.

The world was astounded when Americans Tommie Smith and John Carlos, winners of gold and bronze medals in the 200-meter (218-yard) event, took to the podium with their heads bowed as the national anthem was played. Smith and Carlos took off their shoes as a symbol of black poverty and raised their clenched and gloved fists in a salute associated with the **militant** Black Panther organization.

A dispute broke out immediately, and the IOC demanded that the two athletes be sent home. The U.S. Olympic Committee tried to use Jesse Owens as **mediator.** Owens tried to find a compromise, but he failed and lost his temper in a furious argument.

BLAST AND COUNTERBLAST

Owens expressed his anger over the incident in a book called *Blackthink*, which was co-written with journalist Paul Neimarck and published in 1970. The book criticized the civil rights movement and said that if African Americans failed, it was their own fault. Conservative Americans approved, but criticism poured in from the African–American community.

Owens was genuinely surprised by the reaction to his book. He was persuaded to sit down and read a book called *Soul on Ice* by Eldridge Cleaver, a member of the Black Panther movement. As Owens read Cleaver's book, he realized how far he had come from the cotton fields of Alabama. However, he realized that for most African Americans, poverty and **discrimination** were still a daily reality.

In the early 1970's, Jesse and Minnie Ruth moved to Arizona. There he wrote another book, called *I Have Changed*. In it, he agreed that protest has its place, provided it is non–violent.

FINAL HONORS

By the end of the 1970s, Jesse Owens was at peace with his people and was respected both at home and around the world. In 1972, Ohio State University finally awarded him an honorary degree. In 1974, Owens was given the National Collegiate Athletic Association Theodore Roosevelt Award. In 1976, President Gerald Ford awarded him the Presidential Medal of Freedom. And in 1979, President Jimmy Carter gave Jesse Owens the Living Legend Award.

On March 31, 1980, James Cleveland "Jesse" Owens died in Tucson, Arizona, of lung cancer. He had been smoking heavily for 35 years. Nearly 2,000 people came to his funeral in Chicago. Owens's coffin was draped with the **Olympic** flag.

The five-ringed flag of the Olympic movement is draped over the coffin of Jesse Owens.

In 1981, a contest called the Jesse Owens International Trophy for **amateur** athletes was started. And in 1983, Jesse Owens's name was entered in the U.S. Olympic Hall of Fame. At the opening of the 1984 Olympic Games in Los Angeles, his granddaughter, Gina Hemphill, carried the torch. In 1990, Owens was awarded the Congressional Gold Medal, which was collected by his widow, Minnie Ruth.

Gina Hemphill, Jesse Owens's granddaughter, enters the stadium at the 1984 Olympics.

IN MEMORY

Jesse Owens is still the only athlete ever to have tied or broken five world records in a single day. His most memorable achievement, however, went beyond the track. It took place during the summer of 1936, when he went to Berlin and triumphed in the face of the **Nazis' racism.**

To Jesse Owens, the Olympic ideal was a spiritual one that went far beyond the world of politics. His view was clear: "The road to the Olympics. . . leads to no city, no country. It goes far beyond. . . Nazi Germany. The road to the Olympics leads, in the end, to the best within us."

WHAT PEOPLE SAID ABOUT JESSE OWENS

"Jesse ran so fast I thought my stop-watch was out of order."
> Charles Riley, Owens's coach from 1927-33

"Jesse Owens listens and then he tries to put the suggestions into practice. He is so well coordinated that even a **radical** form change. . . becomes part of his style after a very few practice sessions."
> Larry Snyder, Owens's coach from 1933-36

"[Owens] drew from the stands one of those sudden shouts, high-pitched and accentuated, which the Berlin crowd reserves for a specially popular win."
> *London Morning Post*, August 1936

"Do you really think that I will allow myself to be photographed shaking hands with a **Negro**?"
> Adolf Hitler (as reported by Baldur von Schirach), August 1936

A painting of Jesse Owens in action dwarfs visitors to the 1996 Olympics in Atlanta.

"An American that all Americans should be proud of."

Fiorello H. La Guardia, New York City mayor and early anti-**Nazi** campaigner, 1936

"You were a child, a dark-skinned child, and you knew Jesse Owens before you even knew why. He had been a sprinter and a **broad-jumper,** that much you understood; but there was something more than just his speed that made black folk, even people who cared nothing about sports, swell their chests a little bit at the mention of his name. There was this one time when your house was full, loud with laughter, and a distinguished looking older man appeared on the television screen. 'Isn't that Jesse?' somebody asked. 'Hush, that's Jesse.' And there was silence when Jesse Owens spoke."

Phil Taylor, *Sports Illustrated*, November 29, 1999

JESSE OWENS – TIMELINE

1913 James Cleveland Owens is born in Oakville, Alabama.

1922 The Owens family moves to Cleveland, Ohio. J.C. attends Bolton Elementary School, where he is given the name "Jesse" by mistake.

1927 Jesse is coached by Charles Riley at Fairmount Junior High School.

1930 Jesse goes to Cleveland's East Technical High School.

1932 Relationship with Minnie Ruth Solomon begins. Jesse's first daughter, Gloria, is born. Jesse fails to win a place on the U.S. Olympic team.

1933 National Interscholastic Meet: Jesse ties the world 100-yard (91-meter) sprint record and breaks the 220-yard (201-meter) record. Jesse enrolls at Ohio State University and works part-time at the Ohio State House.

1935 At the Big Ten Championship at Ann Arbor, Michigan, Jesse ties or breaks five world records in one afternoon. Jesse and Minnie Ruth get married.

1936 As a member of the U.S. Olympic team in Berlin. Owens wins four gold medals. After a tickertape parade in New York City, Owens quits amateur sports. Campaigns for Alf Landon.

1937 Owens does exhibition races and makes show-business appearances. His second daughter, Marlene, is born.

1938 Owens's dry-cleaning business collapses.

1940 Owens's parents die. His third daughter, Beverly, is born. Owens enrolls at Ohio State University again.

1941	U.S. enters World War II. Owens runs national physical fitness campaign and goes on to become **personnel officer** for Ford Motors.
1945	End of World War II. Owens starts up a public relations company.
1949	Owens and his family move to Chicago.
1952	Owens becomes Secretary of the Illinois State Athletic Commission.
1956	Owens organizes the Junior Sports Jamboree.
1963	The civil rights movement reaches its peak.
1968	Jesse Owens fails to defuse protest at the Mexico City **Olympic Games.**
1970	Publishes *Blackthink*.
1972	Publishes *I Have Changed*. Awarded honorary degree by Ohio State University.
1976	Awarded Presidential Medal of Freedom.
1980	Jesse Owens dies in Tucson, Arizona.
1981	Jesse Owens International Trophy inaugurated.
1990	Owens is awarded the Congressional Gold Medal.

GLOSSARY

agent someone who is paid a fee to find work for their clients

amateur not professional. An amateur athlete generally does not get paid for competing.

boycott to refuse to take part in or to buy a service as a form of protest

broad-jump long jump

campus grounds of a university

discrimination giving better treatment to people from one group than another

economy way in which business, manufacturing, and employment are organized

establishment existing organization or system

ethnic group group of people who share common descent, language, or culture

genetics scientific study of genes, the units that determine what traits an organism has

heat an opening stage of an athletic event that is used to decide which athletes will compete in the final event

hypocrisy practice of saying one thing but doing another

immigrant person who moves from one country to live in another

integrated allowing people of all races

lucrative very profitable

mediator person who acts as go-between for two fighting people or groups

militant politically aggressive

Nazi member of the National Socialist German Workers' Party, founded after World War I

negro word once used to describe a black person

Olympic Games global sports competition that is held in different cities around the world every four years

Olympic flame flame that symbolizes the Olympic spirit, lit by a torch at the beginning of the Games

Olympic village housing used by athletes and their coaches during the Olympics

persecution harassment or cruelty inflicted upon a person or group of people

personnel officer person who deals with the employees of a firm

pneumonia contagious disease of the lungs

propaganda information put out to persuade people of a political argument

public relations (PR) promotion of goodwill among the public by a company or organization

racism belief that people should be divided according to their race

radical extreme

segregated divided along racial lines

sharecropper tenant farmer who has to pay a share of the crop he grows as rent

slave person who is forced to work without pay

sponsor company that pays people to represent them

swastika ancient symbol of well-being, chosen by the Nazis as an emblem of the so-called "Aryan" race

tickertape white paper ribbons on which news reports were once printed. It used to be showered on parades from New York City offices.

trade union association of workers that aims to protect working conditions and wages

MORE BOOKS TO READ

Hunter, Shaun. *Great African Americans in the Olympics.* New York: Crabtree Publishing Company, 1997.

Nuwer, Hank. *The Legend of Jesse Owens.* Danbury, Conn.: Franklin Watts Incorporated, 1997.

Josephson, Judith Pinkerton. *Jesse Owens: Track & Field Legend.* Berkeley Heights, N.J.: Enslow Publishers, Inc., 1997.

INDEX